WE COME FROM

Kenya

WAMBUI KAIRI

W
HODDER
Wayland

an imprint of Hodder Children's Books

WE COME FROM

Brazil • China • France
Germany • India • Jamaica • Japan
Kenya • Nigeria • South Africa

Many of the people you are about to meet live in a farming village called Kigumo, in Kenya. Like any country, Kenya has many different types of lifestyles. People live in towns and cities as well as the countryside.

Cover: Kiburi and his friends.
Title page (from top to bottom): Nairobi city centre; a metal worker in Nairobi; a giraffe in the Masai Mara game reserve; fishing boats in Mombasa; a Maasai boy with one of his flock of sheep.
Contents page: Kiburi and his schoolfriends playing in their lunch break.
Index: Kiburi and his mum in their back garden.

All Wayland books encourage children to read and help them improve their literacy.

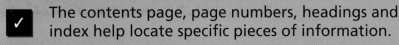 The contents page, page numbers, headings and index help locate specific pieces of information.

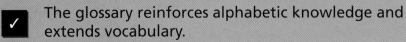 The glossary reinforces alphabetic knowledge and extends vocabulary.

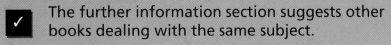 The further information section suggests other books dealing with the same subject.

Series editor: Katie Orchard
Book editor: Philippa Smith
Designer: Jean Wheeler
Production controller: Tracy Fewtrell

Picture Acknowledgements: All the photographs in this book were taken by Gordon Clements. The large map artwork on page 5 was produced by Hardlines. The small world map was produced by Peter Bull.

First published in 1999 by Wayland Publishers Ltd
This edition published in 2002 by Hodder Wayland,
an imprint of Hodder Children's Books
338 Euston Road, London NW1 3BH

British Library Cataloguing in Publication Data
Kairi, Wambui
 We come from Kenya
 1.Kenya - Geography - Juvenile literature
 2.Kenya - Social conditions - 1963 - Juvenile literature
 I.Title II.Kenya
 967'.6'2'042

ISBN 0 7502 4144 6

Typeset by Jean Wheeler, England
Printed and bound in Hong Kong

Contents

Welcome to Kenya!

'My name is Kiburi and this is me with my mother. My older sisters, Wanjiku and Nyamata, are away at boarding school.' Kiburi.

Kiburi is nine years old. He lives with his parents in Kigumo, a farming village to the north of the capital city, Nairobi. You can see where Nairobi is on the map on page 5. You can also see that the Equator runs almost through the middle of Kenya.

▲ *Kiburi and his mother outside their house in Kigumo village.*

Kenya's place in the world.

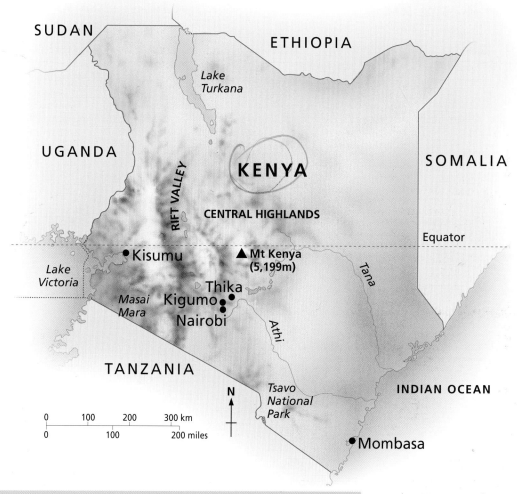

Kenya is in East Africa.

KENYA

Capital city	Nairobi
Land area	582,644 square kilometres
Population	29 million people (1997)
Main language	Kiswahili
Official language	English
Main religion	Christianity

5

The Land and Weather

Kenya is a big, beautiful country in East Africa. It is the home of lions, elephants and black and white zebra.

There are three different types of climate. Much of Kenya is a hot, dry plateau. Part of this is like a desert, where it may rain only once a year.

▶ *The Chania Falls in Thika, in central Kenya.*

▼ *Nairobi city centre. Nairobi is the capital of Kenya.*

'It is very dry on the plateau. We have to walk 10 kilometres to fetch our water.' Mary.

▲ *Early morning mist over Mt Kenya, in the Central Highlands. The top of Mt Kenya has snow and ice all the year round.*

The highlands of the central and Rift Valley region are cool and wet. It is here that most of the food in Kenya is grown. Crops include tea, coffee, potatoes, wheat and barley.

Along the coast it is hot and humid, which is ideal for growing tropical fruits like mangoes, oranges, coconuts and pineapples. This region also attracts many tourists from Europe and the USA.

▶ *Swimming in the warm waters of the Indian Ocean at Mombasa.*

▼ *Impala grazing on the grasslands of the Masai Mara game reserve.*

Home Life

Kiburi lives in Kigumo, a farming village. Here, most families are well off and can afford to have electricity and televisions. Kiburi lives in a nice three-bedroomed house with his parents.

▲ *In Kenya, grandparents often help to look after their grandchildren. This is Kiburi's grandmother and little cousin, Warui.*

▼ *After school, Kiburi feeds the family cows.*

▲ *A city family in their Nairobi flat enjoying television.*

In the cities, some families live in big mansions, but most people live in small flats. Many of them share kitchens and bathrooms with other families.

▶ *Kiburi's mother making* chapatis.

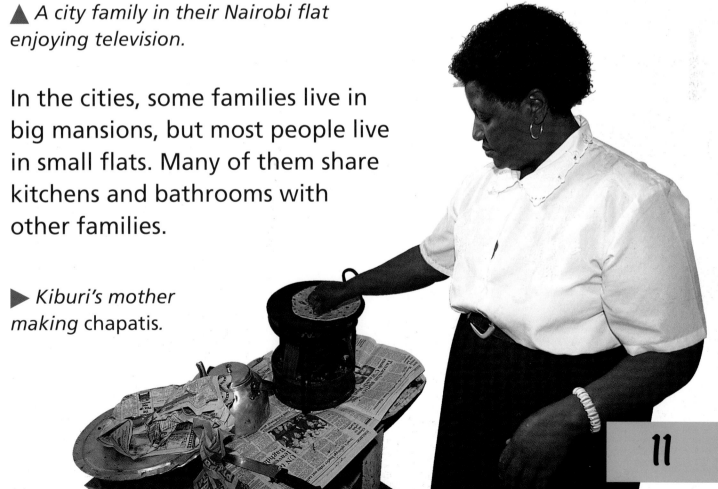

In most country areas the land is owned by families. They live in a compound where many jobs are shared.

Women and young girls do the household work, while men and boys grow the crops and look after the animals.

'I help to look after our sheep and goats to keep them safe from wild animals.' John.

Peter and his family belong to the Maasai tribe. Their home is called a *manyatta*. It is made of cow dung and straw. When it rains the roof is covered with cow skins to keep it dry inside.

Maasai families have no televisions, and only a few have radios. Instead they enjoy singing and dancing.

▲ *Peter and his family outside their* manyatta.

Food and Cooking

Many types of fruit and vegetables are grown in Kenya. They are sold in open markets and supermarkets. People in towns often have vegetable gardens instead of flower gardens.

▼ *Fresh fruit and vegetables for sale in Kigumo village market.*

▲ *A fish market in Mombasa. Seafood is common at the coast, but it is expensive to buy inland.*

▶ *An office worker in Nairobi enjoying traditional Kenyan food at a restaurant.*

Most Kenyans do not have a fridge, so they have to preserve their food. When meat is spiced, or smoked and dried, it keeps for a long time.

15

◀ *Tasty barbecued meat being cooked at a nyama choma* den *in Nairobi.*

▶ *Shopping for beans and rice in Thika.*

Kenyans love meat, especially roast beef and goat. It is known as *nyama choma*, and is usually eaten with salads.

There are *nyama choma* 'dens' (eating places) almost everywhere you go.

'My favourite food is *chapati* and stew.' Kiburi.

16

At Work

In Kigumo, farmers raise cows, chickens and pigs and grow coffee, tea and bananas. They also grow flowers. These are exported to Europe, especially to Britain, Holland and Germany.

'We grow bananas. These are just ready to be harvested.' Kiburi's mum.

In the cities, some people work for the government or in banks, or are doctors or teachers. Others work in factories.

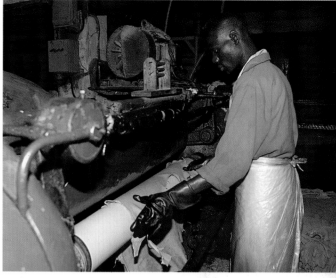

▲ *Preparing animal hides at a leather factory in Thika.*

But most city people work for themselves, often making things from recycled materials. They do this out of doors, which is why this kind of work is called *jua kali* (hot sun).

◀ *A boy in Nairobi recycles old metal pipe to make something new.*

19

At School

In Kenya, children start school at the age of four. When they are six they go to a primary school for eight years. This is followed by four years in high school.

▶ *This is Kiburi's school. The children fetch their cups at break time.*

▼ *Kiburi likes school and sits at the front of his class.*

Kiburi goes to Uncle Musa, a low cost private school in Kigumo village. Here the children learn to write and speak in two languages, English and Kiswahili.

Lessons begin at 8 a.m. and finish at 3.45 p.m. Most schools teach nine subjects. Games, art, music and dance are an important part of school life.

'Today I have Kiswahili and maths homework to do.' Kiburi.

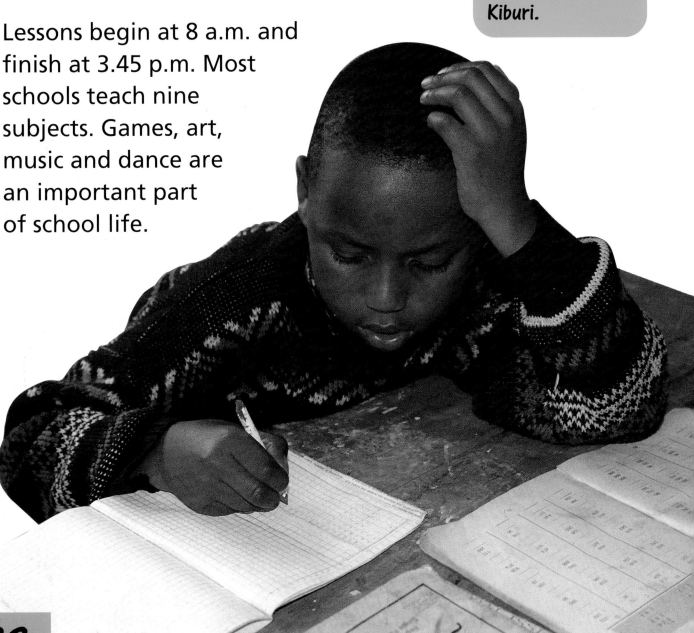

▲ *Children in Thika dancing at Sunday School.*

On Sundays, Christian children go to Sunday school where they pray, sing and play. Muslim children go to Madrasa, a class where they learn the Qu'ran.

▶ *A Nairobi schoolboy waiting for the bus to high school.*

Spare Time

Favourite sports in Kenya are football, *kati* and *bano*. As the weather is usually hot, country children swim in rivers, while those in towns go to swimming pools.

In their free time, Kenyan children are expected to help in the home and look after the farm animals. Many children keep pets, especially dogs and rabbits.

▲ *Children in Nairobi enjoy swimming at the local pool.*

▼ *Feeding giraffes at a wildlife centre on a family day out.*

'We like playing with toys we've made ourselves.' James.

In towns and cities, parents take their children to *nyama choma* dens, where they eat and watch comedians and acrobats.

Looking Ahead

Kenya gained independence in 1963. Since then, Kenyans have worked hard together to build new schools, hospitals and roads.

▲ *New office blocks being built in Nairobi.*

◀ *Maasai women selling bracelets they have made to some of Kenya's many tourists.*

Today, Kenya is a growing centre of trade, tourism and farming. Each year, more tourists come to see the country's wildlife, and in the future Kenya could produce even more food to sell abroad.

'When I grow up I would like to be a doctor.' Kiburi.

Make a *Gakuandi* Toy

Kiburi enjoys making his own toys from recycled materials. This *gakuandi* is made from string and a bottle top.

1. Ask an adult to flatten a bottle top with a hammer and make 2 holes in the middle using a hammer and nail.

2. Take thin string, about 100 cm long, and feed it through one hole and out of the other.

3. Tie the two ends together to make a loop.

4. Put one loop over one forefinger and one loop over the other, leaving the bottle top in the centre of the string.

5. Twirl the string round and round until it twists and tightens on your fingers.

▲ *Kiburi punches two holes in the middle of his bottle top.*

6. Gently pull your hands out sideways until the twisted string begins to unwind. Then let your hands go towards each other as it winds up again.

7. The string will unwind and then rewind more and more as you increase speed.

◀ *Kiburi's* gakuandi *spins faster and faster.*

A large button, about 3 cm across, can be used instead of a bottle top, with strong thread instead of string.

28

Kenya Fact File

◀ **Money Facts**
Kenyan money is the Kenyan shilling. There are 10 cents in one shilling.

River Facts
The longest river in Kenya is the Tana River. It is 708 kilometres long.

▶ **Famous People**
Jomo Kenyatta was Kenya's first President.

▼ **Flag**
The Kenyan flag is black (for black people), red (for the blood that was shed during the fight for independence) and green (for the national heritage).

▼ **Independence Day**
Kenya has a national holiday on 12 December. This is the day when, in 1963, Kenya became independent.

▶ **Wildlife**
In Kenya you can find the lion, elephant, buffalo, rhino and leopard. They are known as 'The Big Five'.

▼ **Stamps**
Many Kenyan stamps have pictures of their beautiful wild birds and animals.

National Parks
The Tsavo National Park is the largest in Kenya. It is 20,800 square kilometres. It contains hundreds of different kinds of animals.

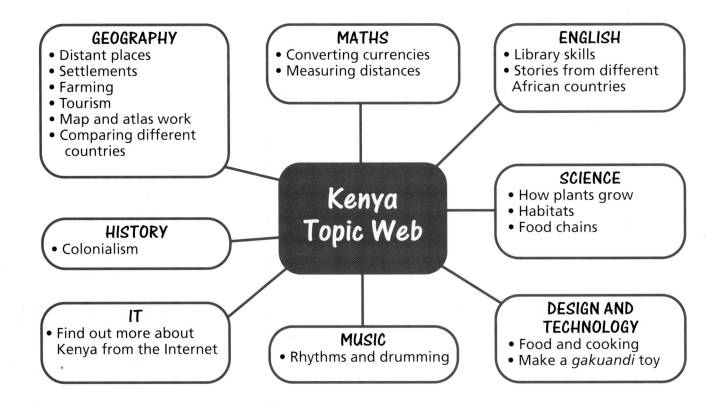

Extension Activities

GEOGRAPHY
- Find out which other countries in the world lie on the Equator.
- Investigate waste and recycling. List the waste produced by the class each week. How could some of it be recycled?

HISTORY
- Find out when and how the Kenya railways were built.
- Find out about the Mau Mau uprising.

DESIGN AND TECHNOLOGY
- Make a collage showing the wild animals that live in Kenya's game reserves.

MUSIC
- Find out about the instruments used to play traditional African music.

MATHS
- Find out how many Kenyan shillings there are in £1 and practise converting the two currencies.

SCIENCE
- Habitats: find out which wild animals live in the Tsavo National Park. Draw examples of the food chains you might find in this habitat.

ENGLISH
- Imagine you are visiting Kenya. Write a postcard describing the weather in the highlands, on the plateau and by the sea.

LITERACY HOUR
- Use this book as an example of non-fiction, and stories from Africa as fiction from other cultures.

Glossary

Bano A marble game for two or more people.

Chapati A type of flat bread, made from wheat.

Compound A group of houses with shared facilities, such as toilets.

Desert A place where it hardly ever rains and very few plants can grow.

Equator An imaginary line around the centre of the Earth, halfway between the north and south poles.

Exported Sold abroad.

Game Reserve A special area of land where wild animals are protected.

Hide Animal skin.

Humid Very damp.

Kati A ball game played by three people.

Plateau A very large and often flat-topped piece of land.

Qu'ran The Muslim Holy Book.

Recycled materials Materials like metals and glass, used again and again to make different things.

Further Information

Fiction:
African Stories retold by Saviour Pirotta (Wayland, 1998)
Misoso: Once Upon a Time Tales From Africa retold by Verna Aardema (Hamish Hamilton, 1995)
Stories from West Africa by Bob Hull (Wayland, 1999)

Non-fiction:
A Flavour of Kenya by Wambui Kairi (Wayland, 1999)
Country Insights: Kenya by Dunne, Kairi & Nyanjom (Wayland, 1997)
Focus on Kenya by Fleur Ng'weno (Evans, 1996)

Organizations:
Kenyan High Commission, 45 Portland Place, London W1N 4AS Tel: 0207 636 2371
Kenya Tourist Office, 25 Brook Mews, London W1Y 1LF Tel: 0207 355 3144

Index

All the numbers in **bold** refer to photographs.